THE CHANGING FACE OF
THE
CARIBBEAN

Text by ALI BROWNLIE
Photographs by JENNY MATTHEWS

HODDER
Wayland

an imprint of Hodder Children's Books

© 2002 White-Thomson Publishing Ltd

Produced for Hodder Wayland by
White-Thomson Publishing Ltd
2/3 St Andrew's Place
Lewes
BN7 1UP

Editor: Aylla Macphail
Designer: Christopher Halls at Mind's Eye Design, Lewes
Proofreader: Alison Cooper
Additional picture research: Glass Onion Pictures Research

First published in Great Britain in 2002 by Hodder Wayland,
an imprint of Hodder Children's Books

This paperback edition published in 2006

British Library Cataloguing in Publication Data
Brownlie, Ali
    The Changing Face of the Caribbean
    1. Caribbean Area
    I. Title II. Caribbean
    972.9

ISBN-10: 0 7502 3853 4
ISBN-13: 978 0 7502 3853 3

Printed and bound in China

Hodder Children's Books
A division of Hodder Headline Limited
338 Euston Road, London NW1 3BH

Acknowledgements

The publishers would like to thank the
following for their contributions to this boo
Nick Hawken – illustration on pages 22, 24,
28, 40, 44; Peter Bull – map on pages 5. All
photographs by Jenny Matthews/ Network
except: Matt Griggs *front cover* (background)
WTP05LB 5 (bottom); HWPL/Gordon
Clements 8 (top and bottom); HWPL 12
(top); HWPL/Howard J Davies 13;
HWPL/Gordon Clements 14; HWPL 24;
HWPL/Howard J Davies 25 (top); HWPL 33
(bottom); HWPL 36. The author would like
to thank Louise Douglas for her help in
researching this book.

Contents

1   Islands in the Sun 4

2   Past Times 6

3   Landscape and Climate.......................8

4   Natural Resources 12

5   The Changing Environment...............16

6   The Changing Population..................20

7   Changes at Home 26

8   Changes at Work 34

9   The Way Ahead 44

Glossary 46

Further Information 47

Index 48

Islands in the Sun

The Caribbean is home to over 36 million people, who have a wide variety of different lifestyles. Each island has its own distinct identity, but there is still much that they share in common. In the past, they have had to overcome difficulties such as slavery and poverty. Today the Caribbean is one of the most popular holiday destinations in the world. In order not to be too general, this book will focus on a small number of islands, in particular, Cuba, Jamaica and Haiti.

The large modern cities and towns of the Caribbean, such as Kingston in Jamaica, Port of Spain in Trinidad and San Juan in Puerto Rico, have theatres, cinemas, sports centres and universities. San Juan has the largest shopping mall in the Caribbean.

A wide range of cultural activities are available, from community theatre to classical ballet, which is particularly popular in Cuba. Several famous writers and poets have come from the Caribbean, including the Nobel prize-winning poet Derek Walcott from St Lucia. Carnivals are celebrated on nearly every island. The Ponce festival is celebrated in every city in Puerto Rico in late February with processions, parades and floats. People wear colourful papier-mâché masks.

Puerto Rico

Dominican Republic

Jamaica

Haiti

Trinidad and Tobago

▲ *A selection of Caribbean national flags.*

◀ *Havana is the capital city and chief seaport of Cuba. It is the largest city in the Caribbean and one of the oldest in the world.*

UNITED
STATES
OF
AMERICA

0   500   1000 km

0   200   400   600 miles

THE
BAHAMAS

Nassau

TURKS & CAICOS
ISLANDS

VIRGIN IS

San
Juan

ANTIGUA &
BARBUDA

MONTSERRAT

GUADELOUPE

DOMÍNICA

MARTINIQUE

ST LUCIA

BARBADOS

Havana

CUBA

G R E A T E R

DOMINICAN
REPUBLIC

HAITI

PUERTO
RICO

ST KITTS
& NEVIS

Port-au-
Prince

Santo
Domingo

N

Montego
Bay

Blue
Mountain

CAYMAN
ISLANDS

Mandeville   Kingston

JAMAICA

A N T I L L E S

ST VINCENT &
THE GRENADINES

ATLANTIC

OCEAN

C A R I B B E A N   S E A

L E S S E R

GRENADA

TRINIDAD &
TOBAGO

Port of
Spain

A N T I L L E S

HONDURAS

ARUBA

NETHERLANDS
ANTILLES

GUYANA

SURINAME

NICARAGUA

V E N E Z U E L A

COSTA
RICA

PANAMA

C O L O M B I A

▲ This map shows the islands and South American countries that make up the Caribbean region.

THE CARIBBEAN: KEY FACTS

Number of islands and states: 11 independent island states, more than 12 dependencies and numerous smaller islands

Population: 36 million (2000 est.)

Largest and most populous island: Cuba (10.8 million)

Most densely populated islands: Barbados (603 per sq km), Puerto Rico (434 per sq km)

Key cities: Havana, Cuba (2.2 million), Kingston, Jamaica (646,400), San Juan, Puerto Rico (455,595)

Main languages: Spanish, English, French

Major religion: Christianity

No one flag represents the Caribbean. This is the Cuban national flag.

2 Past Times

The most striking aspects of Caribbean history are colonialism, slavery, and the resulting struggles for independence. Originally, the islands were inhabited by the Caribs and the Arawaks, also known as the Taínos. They were virtually wiped out by European explorers who colonized most of the islands in the sixteenth century. It is thought that small numbers of Taínos have survived in Puerto Rico, Haiti and Cuba. The Europeans brought slaves from Africa to work on the sugar plantations. Slavery was abolished on most islands at the beginning of the nineteenth century, but workers were still needed, and many came from the Indian subcontinent. Today, the range of languages, religions and peoples to be found in the

◀ A memorial statue of Toussaint L'Ouverture (1744-1803), a slave who led a rebellion against slavery in Haiti. Many Caribbean islands have a proud history of fighting for independence and freedom.

IN THEIR OWN WORDS

'My name is Olga Euphemia Mena and I live in Regla, across the bay from Havana in Cuba. My grandmother was a slave from Africa and she worked on a sugar plantation. Our surname was given to her by her owner. She was freed after the first war of independence against Spain in 1898. She continued to work on the plantation but it was cheaper to hire her by the day than keep her as a slave. Her owner would have had to house her and provide her with food.

'Fidel Castro has been the President of Cuba since 1959. He wants the best for our country but often it's not possible. Many changes are taking place now and we are moving towards democracy. I hope we will be able to go forward.'

Caribbean reflects its history.

Many Caribbean countries remained as colonies of the European nations until they became independent around the 1960s. Puerto Rico became a US commonwealth in 1952. Cuba gained its independence in 1898 when it fought Spain for its freedom from colonial rule. Since independence the islands have developed in different ways. But most countries have continued to have close economic and cultural ties with their former colonial rulers. All of them are increasingly coming under the influence of their near neighbour, the USA.

▲ *These old slave houses in Cuba are waiting to be converted into tourist accommodation. All over the Caribbean there is an increased interest in the region's history.*

3 Landscape and Climate

The Caribbean region is made up of the islands that lie in the Caribbean Sea and the countries of Guyana and Suriname on the South American continent. The islands form a great arc which sweeps south-eastwards from the Gulf of Mexico and then southwards almost to Venezuela. Although many of the islands are small, the Caribbean includes landscapes as different as lush rainforests, mountains, swamps and semi-deserts.

The moving earth

The smaller Caribbean islands are really the tops of huge volcanic mountains that lie beneath the sea. This area is the meeting point of tectonic plates and is therefore prone to earthquakes and volcanoes. Between Cuba and Jamaica there is a 6,000-metre-deep underwater rift valley, formed by the sinking and tearing apart of the Earth's crust.

There are active volcanoes on the islands of St Vincent, Guadeloupe and Montserrat. The volcano on Montserrat began to erupt in 1995, forcing half the population to leave the island. Many of the other islands have old volcanic craters and hot springs. On St Lucia it is possible to drive into the crater of an old volcano and on Dominica there is a 'boiling lake', heated from deep inside the earth's surface.

▲ The Petite Piton mountain in St Lucia is all that is left of a volcanic mountain. This is known as a 'volcanic plug'.

Rivers and waterfalls

The Caribbean islands are typically mountains surrounded by low, flat coastal plains. Fast rivers flow off the mountains and tumble over rocky waterfalls where the land falls steeply. The mountain sides are often heavily wooded. There are rainforests in areas where the rainfall is high.

◄ As the streams rush from the mountains to the sea they create waterfalls like these Diamond Falls in St Lucia.

IN THEIR OWN WORDS

'I am Ezekiel McGowan. I am 34 years old and I have two children. I wear this hard hat to protect me from the sun. I have a job, but I also have my own small piece of land on Blue Mountain in Jamaica. I grow coffee, bananas, pineapples, mangoes and vegetables. I sell the produce locally here on Blue Mountain.

'It is very difficult to grow things here. The hillside is steep and the rain washes all the good soil away. So I have cut terraces, or steps, into the hillside and planted bamboo, which holds on to the soil. It's hard work going up and down the hill all the time. I would like my children to do something else when they are older – farming is too hard.'

▲ *Farming is difficult on the steep hillsides of Jamaica's Blue Mountain.*

A tropical climate

All parts of the Caribbean have a similar tropical climate, although there are some local differences. The hottest time is from June to August, with temperatures reaching 30 °C. In the mountains and hills it is much cooler than this. From December to March it is less hot, but with average temperatures still over 20 °C, and low rainfall, this is the time when most tourists like to visit.

Wind and rain

Trade winds blow all year from the north-east and these keep the temperatures cooler in places like St Vincent and the Dominican Republic. It is these winds that bring much of the rain to the Caribbean and this usually falls on the north or east coasts of the islands, making them greener than the drier south or west coasts. The rainy season is expected on most islands during September and October. Haiti and Cuba have two short rainy seasons in April and October but both islands also suffer from occasional droughts.

▲ *The Caribbean is famous for its year-round pleasant climate.*

◀ *When it rains in the Caribbean it can rain very heavily. Even so, children still have to go to school.*

Stormy weather

Most of the Caribbean lies in the path of tropical storms and hurricanes that can batter the islands with strong winds and torrential rain at any time between July and October. Trinidad and Tobago escapes the hurricanes because they pass by to the north.

There is some evidence that the Caribbean climate is changing. In some areas rainfall has decreased since 1970 by over 20 per cent, dry spells are longer and temperatures have risen by 1 per cent. Hurricanes have become more unpredictable and fiercer. Global warming and deforestation are possible reasons for this.

▲ On the south coast of Jamaica rainfall is much lower and the vegetation is more sparse.

IN THEIR OWN WORDS

'My name is Paulette Boisie and I live in Fonds Verrette in Haiti. I lost half my house to Hurricane George. The wind and rain grew stronger and stronger. We decided to leave in the night and had to struggle through the storm to shelter on the hill. A great river of water poured through the village, bringing huge rocks down and sweeping away everything in its path.

'Most of the church was destroyed and 140 houses. Eighty-five people died, but my family all survived. We've lost everything though, including all our fruit trees and vegetable plants. There's no road out of here now. Everything is covered in mud, and these boulders make it impossible for cars to get through.'

Natural Resources

The Caribbean is not a region rich in natural mineral resources. Oil and natural gas in Trinidad and Tobago, bauxite in Jamaica and Guyana, and copper and limestone in Puerto Rico are the notable exceptions. Most Caribbean countries have to import oil from other countries, which is very expensive for them. They need the oil to fuel their increasing numbers of cars and factories.

Oil and natural gas

Trinidad and Tobago has become one of the richest nations in the Caribbean because of its reserves of oil and gas. It started producing oil in 1908. The oil industry was nationalized in the 1970s. This ensures that the country benefits from the oil business, instead of the profits going to private companies. Production is still increasing, with 150,000 barrels of oil produced a day in 2000. Of this, 130,00 barrels were exported, mainly to the USA and Latin America.

▲ *Most of the energy needs of the Caribbean are met by imports. These storage tanks in Antigua are filled with liquid propane imported from the USA.*

IN THEIR OWN WORDS

'My name is Velroy McKenzie and I am 17 years old. I live near Mandeville in Jamaica. My dad is in charge of all the workers and machines at a bauxite mine. I sometimes watch the lorries taking the bauxite to the port. It takes a lot of energy to turn bauxite in to aluminium, so the bauxite is shipped to places like Canada where they have cheap electricity. If we could process the bauxite in Jamaica we would make a lot more money. I would like to work in the mine when I'm older but my dad says there will be fewer jobs if the price of bauxite goes down.'

Barbados also produces a small amount of oil. Natural gas, which is found alongside the oil, is a more environmentally friendly energy source. It is beginning to replace oil as Trinidad and Tobago's most important natural resource. Cars on the island run on natural gas.

Red gold

Jamaica has vast reserves of bauxite and is the world's third largest producer. Bauxite accounts for half of Jamaica's export income. Guyana was also famous for its bauxite in the 1970s. Production has dropped dramatically since then, but it still accounts for over 35 per cent of Guyana's export earnings. Bauxite is formed in volcanic rocks, such as basalt, and is used to make aluminium. Aluminium is a strong and very light metal used to make aeroplanes, aircraft engines, cars, machinery, boats, pots, pans and cans.

◀ *Bauxite is a key export for Jamaica, but ore prices are falling.*

Alternative energy

Oil is a fossil fuel that is not sustainable. This means that we are using it up at a much faster rate than nature can replace it. Nearly 90 per cent of the Caribbean's energy needs are met by fossil fuels. Several countries have recognized the importance of finding their own sources of energy that are more environmentally friendly.

St Lucia is investigating the possibility of developing energy from the heat given off by hot volcanic springs inside the volcano. This is known as 'geothermal energy'. Guyana and the Dominican Republic are among the islands planning hydroelectric plants on some of their rivers. Puerto Rico has dammed some of its rivers for hydroelectric power, but this meets only 2 per cent of its energy needs. The Caribbean sunshine makes solar energy an obvious option. But it is very expensive to set up and, as yet, it is not used on a large scale.

▼ *These smoking hot sulphuric springs at Soufrière are a possible source of geothermal energy for St Lucia.*

◄ *Jamaica has over 2,000 solar water heaters and Barbados has over 26,000.*

Fish

Fish have been one of the main natural sources of food for people in the Caribbean for centuries. But the fish stocks have started to decline dramatically. Between 1977 and 1985 fish catches dropped by 30 per cent and then dropped by another 38 per cent between 1985 and 1990. Population growth and tourism have increased demand for fish and also increased pollution levels. Oil slicks are created by passing ships that dump their engine waste. These slicks destroy the coral reefs and kill the fish. Artificial reefs and marine parks to protect the fish are being established by nearly all of the islands.

IN THEIR OWN WORDS

'My name is Gladstone McFarlane and I'm a fisherman from Jamaica. I work in a crew of three and we catch sprat and snapper fish. We have a small boat with an outboard motor, which we take just a few miles out from the shore. When we come back from a fishing trip, the vendors come and buy from us. Sometimes we catch enough to live off, sometimes it's hard. My sons don't want to be fishermen.

'There's much more pollution here now. Many of the ships discharge a black oil which kills the fish and the big companies in the free trade zone (*see page 36*) dump their waste into the sea, which is bad for fishing.'

5 The Changing Environment

The Caribbean is famous for its striking scenery and abundant plant and animal life. There are important areas of swamp in Jamaica and Trinidad. They provide homes to birds such as the scarlet ibis, herons and egrets. Rare species, including parrots, turtles, flamingos and alligators, are found in various parts of the Caribbean. The coqui tree frog is found almost nowhere else in the world apart from Puerto Rico. There are thousands of exotic flowers, including wild orchids and hibiscus.

But these natural habitats are threatened by the changes that are taking place in the Caribbean. The growth in population and number of tourists means that more land is being developed to accommodate them. Towns are expanding and traffic is increasing. More factories are being built and modern farming methods are being used. These developments are resulting in serious pollution problems which could be disastrous for the wildlife of the region.

Tourism and the environment

Tourism brings in money from other countries and creates jobs, but it can be very harmful to the environment. The aeroplanes that bring people to and from the islands are causing increasing air pollution problems. New hotels, airports and roads have to be built. The flat land that is suitable for building on is scarce

▲ The Caribbean's beautiful flora could be damaged by increasing development and industrialization.

◄ The increase in cars in Kingston, Jamaica has led to traffic jams and serious air pollution.

on many islands. This has resulted in precious areas of forest being cleared, destroying fragile habitats and wildlife.

More tourists create more sewage which, if it goes into the sea untreated, can kill the inshore fish and damage the coral reefs. Governments are building new sewage systems and introducing conservation programmes to deal with these problems.

▶ *Havana harbour in Cuba has suffered from serious pollution. A clean-up operation is proving successful as fish are now returning to the bay.*

IN THEIR OWN WORDS

'My name is Courtenay Black and I work as a marine park ranger for the Negril Coral Reef Preservation Society. This was set up in 1998 after a long battle to make people realize that the coral reef was being destroyed. We believe that as much as half of it has already been lost. Now we are taking action to reverse that.

'Our job is to analyse the river water that flows down to the sea to discover where the problems are. Lots of activities on the land can pollute the sea. They include sewage outflow, deforestation, and pesticide and fertilizer run-off from farmland. I test for chemicals in the seawater, such as nitrates, phosphates and ammonia. Sewage levels have increased a lot because there are so many new hotels in the area. A new sewage system is improving the situation.'

Poverty and the environment

Haiti is one of the poorest countries in the world. Local people have had to make use of whatever they can find in order to survive. Trees have been cut down for fuel and so that food can be grown on the cleared land. Huge areas of rainforest have been lost, and in 2000 only 5 per cent of Haiti's original rainforest was remaining.

The lack of trees means that when it rains the soil is easily washed away. Nothing can be grown on the rocky ground that remains. As each year goes by the amount of land that is suitable for growing crops is shrinking. The problem is at its worst in Haiti but the situation is similar on other Caribbean islands where there are poor people, steep slopes and heavy rains. The only real solution is to reduce poverty so that people can survive without damaging the environment.

▲ *Haiti is one of the most deforested countries in the world.*

IN THEIR OWN WORDS

'My name is Claire Hyppolyte and I live in Vielle Terre in Haiti. I work on a soil conservation project. I work for six days a week. I am paid for five days and work another day for free.

'When it rains here, the water runs down to the sea, taking the good topsoil with it. All the hard work people have put into cultivating the land is simply washed away. Experts believe that in five to ten years' time nothing will be able to grow here. So we are building retaining walls around the plots so that the soil will not be washed away when it rains. Where the walls have been built, the rains are no longer destroying people's hard work. Instead, they help the gardens grow and give people food.'

Industrial damage

Bauxite is mined in Jamaica by opencast mining. This means that the bauxite is dug out directly from the surface and there is no need for underground mining. Opencast mining destroys the landscape and can be very bad for the environment. For every tonne of bauxite mined, a tonne of waste is produced, which is then pumped into nearby lakes. The waste contains caustic acid which kills the wildlife in the lakes.

▼ *This lake has turned red because of the waste from the bauxite mines that has been pumped into it.*

Several steps have been taken to make bauxite mining less harmful to the environment. The mining companies now have to remove the topsoil before they start work. The soil is saved so that it can be used to restore the landscape when mining in the area is finished. The mining companies themselves have set up sanctuaries to preserve wild orchids found growing in mining areas. They have also started tree-planting schemes to replace the 5,000 hectares that have been lost since they started mining 50 years ago.

▲ *The bauxite mining company has restored this land to farmland now that they have finished mining here.*

The Changing Population

Different peoples

A unique mix of people whose ancestors came from all over the world live in the Caribbean region. The races have intermingled and lived side by side for hundreds of years. They have created new and vibrant cultures which are a mixture of African, Indian, Chinese, Arabic and European influences. Each group of people has added something of their own culture to the food and cooking, music, culture and religions of the Caribbean.

European impact

In Cuba and Puerto Rico about 60 per cent of the people are white or mixed-race descendants of Spanish people. But on most islands, black Afro-Caribbeans make up the majority of the population. They are descended from the millions of slaves brought from Africa by the Europeans to work on the sugar plantations.

After slavery was abolished in the nineteenth century, cheap labour was still needed. People came to work in the Caribbean from India, China, Portugal and Brazil. Today, Guyana and Trinidad and Tobago both have large Indian

▲ Jamaica is a multicultural society made up primarily of people of African origin. Its national motto is 'Out of many, one people'.

◄ About two-thirds of the Cuban population are descended from Spanish people.

populations (over 40 per cent of the Trinidadian population). Havana, in Cuba, has its own Chinatown inhabited by descendants of the Chinese workers who came to work on the sugar plantations in the 1800s.

White people in the Caribbean come from a variety of backgrounds. In Puerto Rico and Cuba, many are descended from Spanish settlers. A few are the descendants of the original plantation owners. Some are descended from people who came to the Caribbean in the nineteenth and early twentieth centuries in search of a better life. Their home countries included Scotland, Ireland, Spain and France.

▲ Most Haitians (95 per cent) are of African descent.

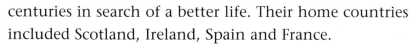

IN THEIR OWN WORDS

'My name is Georgia Balfour and I live in Spanish Town, which is close to Kingston, Jamaica. My ancestors came from Africa. The Caribbean is a very multicultural place, which gives its culture a lively and exciting feel. It's also a good place to live and work. I'm doing a degree in Business Management and I also work in retail sales.

'I'm thinking of doing a Master's degree when I finish this course because the job market is so competitive. I am a very motivated person and my dream is to become an entrepreneur. I think I have the skills I need to lead others. When you work for someone else you don't see all the benefits.'

Growing population

By 2000, the population of the Caribbean was approximately 36 million. That figure is almost double the population in 1960. It is estimated that by 2025 it will increase to 45 million. The population is still growing, but at a slower rate. The slow down is because women are becoming more educated and they are choosing to have smaller families.

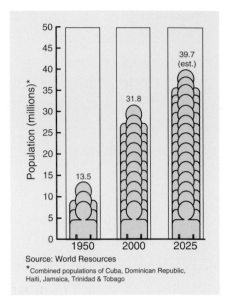

Source: World Resources

*Combined populations of Cuba, Dominican Republic, Haiti, Jamaica, Trinidad & Tobago

▲ *Look at the steady growth in this sample section of the Caribbean population.*

◄ *People are living longer and the number of elderly people is rising in most Caribbean countries.*

The continued growth of the Caribbean population is largely due to health improvements. In 2000, people lived to an average age of 69 in the Caribbean. This figure is a little misleading as it ranges from 78 years in Martinique, Cuba and Dominica, to only 49 in Haiti. The differences in life expectancy between the islands are due to the different levels of poverty that people have to overcome.

The number of babies who survive early childhood is also increasing. In some Caribbean countries, the number of babies that die before they reach the age of one has halved since 1975. In Haiti, where many people live in extreme poverty, it is still very high. In the year 2000, for every thousand babies born there, 82 died before their first birthday. This is in sharp contrast to the rate of survival in richer countries. In Cuba, for instance, the figure was only nine.

HIV/AIDS

The health of the Caribbean population is threatened by the rapid increase in the number of people with HIV/AIDS. The Caribbean now has the second-highest incident rate for HIV/AIDS after Africa. In 1995 there were just over 8,000 AIDS cases. By 2000 this number had risen to 28,000. In the future the cost of caring for people with the virus will require an increasing amount of funding. Some estimates warn that the whole health programme budget in some countries will have to be spent dealing with AIDS.

▲ *Haiti has a young population, with nearly 60 per cent under the age of 25.*

IN THEIR OWN WORDS

'My name is Maite Ramirez. I'm 34 and I am a doctor in Havana, Cuba. Health is a priority for the Cuban government and they spend a lot of money making sure that everyone has free health care. If people have to go into hospital, or if they need medicines, they do not have to pay. Young children are vaccinated against certain diseases, such as meningitis B. Some of the work I do is on health education, helping people to have healthy lifestyles so that they don't get ill in the first place. Doctors are only paid a basic salary, but it is enough. I am proud to be a doctor.'

Moving around the Caribbean

Migration between the islands is common in the Caribbean. The richer islands draw workers from less wealthy islands nearby. Trinidad, with jobs in the oil industry, is a popular destination for people from nearby Grenada, St Vincent and St Lucia. Each year many Haitians go across the border to the Dominican Republic to cut the sugar cane.

Migration to urban areas is rapidly increasing and over 60 per cent of the Caribbean population now live in towns or cities. Cities, such as Kingston and San Juan, are popular because they offer jobs and better education opportunities. This movement to the cities is unplanned and there are growing problems with housing and transportation.

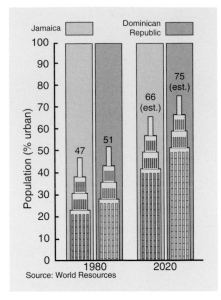

▲ *The percentage of people who live in towns and cities in the Caribbean is expected to grow rapidly by 2020.*

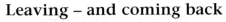

◄ *This bus goes on the ferry between St Kitts and Nevis. Passengers go to visit families and to look for work.*

Leaving – and coming back

Many Caribbean people emigrated to Britain in the 1950s to help to rebuild the country after the Second World War. In the 1980s, new immigration laws were brought in which made it very difficult for people to emigrate to Europe.

The USA and Canada then became the most popular destinations for Caribbean emigrants. Two million Puerto Ricans have moved to the USA, and there are now more Jamaicans in New York than in the whole of Europe. Some people, unhappy with the way the governments in Cuba and Haiti are running their countries, have tried to get to the USA illegally by boat. There is a large community of Cubans in Miami, USA.

▲ *Many people are leaving the Caribbean to look for work abroad.*

Many of the people who leave the Caribbean are young people hoping to study. Unfortunately, it is often the well-educated, or the most motivated people, who go abroad. These are the people that the Caribbean needs if it is to develop and be successful in the future.

Some people who emigrated to Europe in the 1950s and 1960s are now returning to retire in the sunshine and warmth of the Caribbean. Many Puerto Ricans have also come back from the USA, because there have not been enough job opportunities.

IN THEIR OWN WORDS

'My name is Dwayne Mohan. I am 17 years old and I live in Kingston, Jamaica. I have wanted to be a doctor ever since I was a young child. It's a chance to help others and you get paid well. I will probably have to go to the USA to study medicine. I already have a lot of family there. They have been sending money back to help pay for my education. I may come back to work here for a while, but I will probably leave eventually. I can't look to Jamaica for a future. There are more opportunities abroad.'

Rich and poor

The gap between rich and poor is widening on most islands of the Caribbean. In Haiti, 80 per cent of the population live in extreme poverty while a small number of people are exceptionally rich. In Cuba, there is not such a big gap between the rich and the poor, although many people find it difficult to make enough money to live comfortably.

◀ *Shanty towns are common on the outskirts of towns. This one in Haiti is next to a rubbish tip.*

IN THEIR OWN WORDS

'My name is Susan Melbourne. I'm 18 and I live in Kingston, Jamaica. The US influence is changing the way we live here. We still listen to our own music – especially reggae – but we hear a lot of US sounds as well. The children are all inside watching US television. Sometimes they don't even know who their neighbours are any more.

'Most of the clothes we wear come from the US. Many of them are actually made here in the factories in the free trade zone (*see page 36*). The finished products are sent to the US and then they are sold back to us. We are forgetting our own designers. Even with shoes, if you're not wearing a fashionable brand name, you're not wearing anything.'

The influence of the USA

In many ways the USA is replacing the influence that the European countries once had on the Caribbean. Many of the tourists to the Caribbean are from the USA and Canada. US television programmes are beamed directly to most Caribbean islands. Even in Cuba, where there is no access to US television, the country is so close to the US mainland that they can receive US radio. People in the Caribbean watch news programmes which concentrate on events in the USA. They see advertisements for goods, such as clothes and computer games, that are not available in the Caribbean, or that they cannot afford.

Many young people have begun to follow a lifestyle that is more American than Caribbean. They often want to go to the USA to see what it is really like. Some people do not allow their children to watch television because they want their children to grow up learning about Caribbean culture and to play an active part in their own communities.

◄ *US-style modern shopping malls are now a feature of many Caribbean towns.*

Education

Education is highly valued in the Caribbean. Its importance in securing a good job is well recognized. Schools are often very crowded, with over 40 children in a class. The numbers of children going to school, and the length of time they stay there, has risen steadily since 1970. As a result, the number of adults who can read and write has risen. In Cuba the literacy rate has increased from 92 per cent in 1980 to 98 per cent in 2000. In the Dominican Republic the literacy rate for the same period has gone from 74 per cent to 84 per cent. The situation is not so positive in poorer countries like Haiti where many parents cannot afford the uniform or the books they need to send their children to school.

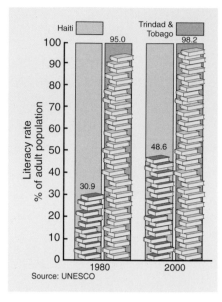

Source: UNESCO

▲ *The percentage of adults who can read and write has increased dramatically in these countries.*

◄ *The number of girls staying on at school is rising across the Caribbean.*

Families

Almost one-third of Caribbean homes have a woman as the head of the household. Some people in the Caribbean live in extended families, with grandparents, aunts and uncles all living together or very nearby. Old people are looked after by their families rather than going into special homes for the elderly.

Caribbean family sizes are getting smaller as people decide to have fewer children. The decrease is most dramatic in Haiti where the average number of children for each woman has dropped from six in 1980 to just under three in 2000.

IN THEIR OWN WORDS

'My name is Raymond Jean. I am 13 years old and I live in Bleck in Haiti. I am working on my parents' coffee plantation, picking the ripe beans, then washing and drying them. My parents have paid for me to start the second year of primary school but they don't have enough money to buy me a uniform yet. The school does not allow you in without a uniform. Sometimes I work for other farmers and I get paid for that. I don't spend the money. I give it to my mum. I also help my mum by collecting the water every day.'

With increasing numbers of women going out to work, family life is changing throughout the Caribbean.

Food

Traditional Caribbean foods include fresh fish, rice and fruit, such as mangoes and pineapples, which are in plentiful supply across the Caribbean. But eating habits in the Caribbean are becoming more and more Westernized. The healthy traditional foods are being replaced by fast foods such as hamburgers and chips. There has been a rise in cancer cases in recent years and this could be linked to changes in diet. Forty per cent of the Caribbean population were overweight in 2000, compared with only 12 per cent in the 1970s.

▶ *In rural areas people often grow their own food. Here, in Haiti, the women are preparing plantain, which are usually sliced and fried.*

Sport and leisure

Cricket and baseball are the most popular sports in the Caribbean. Cricket was originally brought to the West Indies by the English but is now firmly established as a traditional West Indian sport. The West Indies cricket team is internationally renowned for its world class cricket. US sports are also very popular. Baseball and basketball are favourites amongst young people and many are choosing to play them in preference to cricket.

Much of the leisure time of young people now involves modern technology. Satellite television attracts large Caribbean audiences and many young people also spend hours on computer games. More and more Internet cafés are being set up where people can surf the web and email their friends in other countries.

▲ *In Cuba baseball is the national sport. It is becoming more popular in other islands too.*

▼ *This cyber café in Jamaica offers telephone and email services.*

Culture

Music is at the heart of Caribbean culture, whether it is reggae in Jamaica, calypso in Trinidad, or salsa in Cuba. Cuban music has enjoyed great popularity in Europe and the USA in recent years. But many young Cubans, in common with other young people in the Caribbean, often prefer listening to pop music.

Story-telling has also been an important part of Caribbean culture. The Anansi stories of Jamaica and the Tim-Tim stories in St Lucia are based on traditional African stories that the slaves brought with them. There is concern today that the art may die out because children prefer watching television to being told stories. In St Lucia the tales are sometimes still told in Creole, which is a language that few children are able to understand.

IN THEIR OWN WORDS

'My name is Felix Martinez. I am 54 years old and I am a musician in Cuba. I've been playing music since I was 5 years old. I am in a band called Los Candelas and we play country music. We've toured many countries, including Canada, Spain, Poland and Italy. Cuban music is at the peak of its popularity at the moment. It is known throughout the world. The traditional music from the 1920s to 1940s is coming back, but with a new edge to it. More people are listening to our music, and more tourists are coming to the country. It's great for us as a band, and it's great for Cuba.'

Religion

Religion plays a very important part in most people's lives in the Caribbean. The major religion is Christianity – mainly Roman Catholicism in the islands that were colonized by the Spanish, such as Puerto Rico, and the French, such as Haiti. Protestantism is the main religion in islands the English colonized. In 1996, the Anglican Church in Jamaica was the first in the Caribbean to ordain women into its priesthood.

Many other religions are followed, including Hinduism (particularly in Trinidad and Tobago), Islam, Rastafarianism, and other traditional African religions. Religion was banned in Cuba until 1990, but its popularity there has been growing steadily since then. Many people in Cuba follow *Santeria*, which is a mixture of Catholicism and African religions.

A strong community

Life has changed very little for people living in rural areas. Community life is still very important. People know each other well and help each other when they have problems. Evenings are often spent sitting outside, chatting about the events of the day and exchanging local gossip. As television comes to more villages, and young people leave for the towns and cities this way of life may begin to change.

◄ *A streetside game of dominoes is always popular in Cuba.*

IN THEIR OWN WORDS

'My name is Horace Levy and I live in Kingston, Jamaica. The inner city has problems that the rest of society needs to know about. Politicians promise inner-city people a better life in order to get their vote and then they ignore them. People need respect. A recent survey of children showed that they consider respect more important than anything else, even more important than jobs. 'Respect' is the word we use when we say goodbye. We still have a strong sense of community here that comes from our African roots. We have to look after each other. Jamaica has no social security system to help the poor people and the unemployed.'

Life in the cities

The sense of community is already being threatened in the towns and cities. People have busier working lives and they no longer have time to get to know their neighbours. For the successful people who have well paid jobs, city life is good. There are modern shopping malls and good electricity and tap water supplies. But in the shanty towns on the edges of the cities, and in some of the inner-city areas, facilities are poor, crime rates are high and life is hard.

Jamaica has one of the highest murder rates in the world. This may result from the high unemployment levels among young people. But many Jamaicans believe that the rise in violent crime is due to a breakdown in traditional family and moral values. In areas with large Rastafarian populations, family ties remain strong and people lead much more peaceful lives.

▼ *These Rastafarians live in Jamaica. Rastafarians believe in non-violence and have strong family values.*

8 Changes at Work

Farming has traditionally been the main source of work in the Caribbean. But now more and more people are working in the manufacturing and service industries, such as tourism and information technology.

Foreign influence

The Caribbean is heavily dependent upon countries like the USA for the success of its countries' economies. Puerto Rico has benefited greatly from US investment since the 1950s. Foreign firms often come to the Caribbean because people will work for less than in the USA or other Western countries. Many of the region's factories, information technology companies and hotels are owned by US companies. Jamaica's bauxite mines are owned by US and European companies. Changes in the world bauxite or oil prices, over which the Caribbean countries have no control, can also seriously affect the economies of Jamaica and Trinidad and Tobago.

◄ *Satellite dishes help businesses in the Caribbean to communicate with the rest of the world.*

IN THEIR OWN WORDS

'I'm Garth Abiola and I live in Kingston, Jamaica. I did a Master's degree in electronic data systems in the USA. I learned all about information technology and computers. The Jamaican business environment has taken a turn for the worse recently. We're experiencing a decline in business growth because of a downturn in the US economy. When the US sneezes Jamaica catches a cold. We tend to depend on the US too much. Jamaica has a lot going for it – tourism, beautiful people, the island itself. There are some smart people here but the country doesn't always give them a chance.'

The electronic age

Many new jobs in data-processing have been created since the early 1990s. This work involves inputting information into computers for foreign firms including airlines, banks and insurance companies. Satellite links are used to send and receive the information. The main data-processing centres are in Barbados and Jamaica, and there are smaller centres in Trinidad, Grenada, St Kitts and the Dominican Republic.

◀ *Computers and other modern office equipment are common in most Caribbean islands.*

More factories

The Caribbean's manufacturing industry has grown dramatically since the 1980s. Many countries have had to attract overseas companies to set up factories because they cannot afford to build their own. Free trade zones have been established in countries with high unemployment, such as the Dominican Republic, Jamaica and St Lucia.

◀ *These women in St Lucia are working in a factory making underwear. The factory is owned by a foreign company.*

The free trade zones attract foreign companies because they do not have to pay tax and the rent is cheap. They also pay very low salaries – in some cases just 10 per cent of what they would have to pay if their factories were in the developed world. Companies from the USA, Canada and UK have factories in the free trade zones. More recently, companies from the Far East have also become involved. The factories make clothes, electronic products and processed food. The goods are produced for sale abroad and are not available on the islands where they are made.

IN THEIR OWN WORDS

'My name is Alicia Brown and I'm from Kingston, Jamaica. For several years now I have worked in the clothes factory in the free trade zone. The free trade zone is almost like another country. The whole area is closed off and we are searched before we can go in. I tag and pack sweaters that will eventually be sold in New York. My work is very repetitive. I start work at eight in the morning and finish at four in the afternoon. I am happy to have this job because it is hard to find work in Jamaica.'

The role of women

Women's working lives have changed greatly since the 1960s. They have traditionally been the ones to do the farming and housework. Now only 13 per cent of women work in agriculture. Women are becoming more educated. In 2000, for the first time, more women were at university than men. Women work in factories and offices, in the new data-processing industries, and as doctors and teachers. About 90 per cent of the free trade zone workers are women. The number of female politicians is increasing faster in the Caribbean than almost anywhere else in the world. However, women's average earnings are still lower than men's.

▶ *This woman is a peanut farmer in Haiti, where there are fewer job opportunities.*

Farming

In most Caribbean countries, the number of people working in agriculture is falling. Modern machinery means that fewer people are needed to work the land, and more jobs are being created in the service industries and manufacturing. In 1979, agriculture made up over 15 per cent of St Lucia's income. By 1999 this had dropped to just over 7 per cent. In Haiti, however, over 70 per cent of the population still have to depend on the land to survive.

Cash crops

Crops produced for export are called cash crops. The main cash crops of the Caribbean are sugar, citrus fruit, coffee, bananas and tobacco (in Cuba). In the past, cash crops have been produced on big plantations. The plantations have recently been divided into smaller plots of land and sold to local farmers. It is often very difficult for Caribbean farmers to earn a living from the land. World prices for many cash crops have fallen and the farmers do not control the prices they are paid for their produce.

▲ *This man in Haiti is loading sorghum on to his donkey. Sorghum is a grain that is used to feed both humans and animals.*

◄ *Young children often have to work to help their families. This girl is picking coffee beans.*

The case of bananas

Bananas have been a main source of income for many Caribbean islands for several years. The smaller islands of the eastern Caribbean such as St Vincent and St Lucia are particularly dependent on the banana trade. Caribbean farmers have been given guaranteed prices for their bananas by Europe because of the historical connection with the islands.

The USA has argued that the Caribbean farmers should compete with the US-owned banana plantations in Central America. Bananas are usually grown in the Caribbean on small, family-run farms. These farmers cannot compete with the cheaper fruit available from Central America and many are finding it very hard to stay in business.

IN THEIR OWN WORDS

'My name is Claire Turner. I live with my husband Roger on our banana farm in Jamaica. We were both born here. Roger's family came from Scotland 200 years ago. The banana trade is very tough at the moment. We have to produce a better banana for a lower price. We would like to produce organic bananas but the warm, humid conditions that bananas need are also just what bugs like, so we have to use quite a lot of chemicals. We only export the best bananas. The rest are sold locally to the higglers. Nothing is wasted – the banana leaves are spread on the fields as mulch and the damaged fruit is fed to the cattle.'

Tourism

The Caribbean tourist trade has been growing rapidly over recent years. More people have been travelling to the region from richer parts of the world, such as North America and Europe. Throughout the Caribbean, this increase in tourism is creating new jobs, including cleaners, waiters, security guards and tour guides.

Special duty-free shopping centres have been developed in Barbados, the US Virgin Islands and St Lucia. Tourists can buy the latest foreign fashions and high quality goods in these centres without having to pay tax. No items made by local people are sold through these centres.

Whole towns and villages have been enriched by tourism. Ocho Rios, on the north coast of Jamaica, is the country's most popular cruise ship destination. In the early 1960s, it was a small fishing village, typical of many Caribbean villages. Today, it is a town with shops, American chain hotels and a population of over 13,000.

Cruise ships that sail around the Caribbean are becoming increasingly popular with holiday makers. But this does not always benefit the islands because the tourists only come ashore for a short time. They spend most of their money on board the ship.

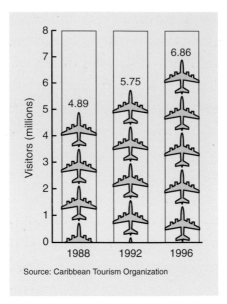

Source: Caribbean Tourism Organization

▲ *Every year, more people are travelling to the Caribbean.*

IN THEIR OWN WORDS

'My name is Alexis Naranjo. I am 35 years old and I live in Havana, Cuba. I've been working at the Hotel Naçional for the last seven years. It's a great job. Big changes are taking place in Havana. The government is spending some of the money brought in by tourism on improving the city. Old Havana was pretty destroyed but now it's been renovated. The old hotels have been done up and each year there are an extra 5,000 beds available. We used to have only German, Italian and Spanish tourists. Now people come from many more places – France, Finland, Holland and Canada.'

Eco-tourism is also growing in popularity. People come to see the extraordinary wild animals and plants of the Caribbean. This has brought tourism to areas away from the coasts and created more jobs in rural areas.

Tourism on some islands, particularly Jamaica, can be badly affected by reports of crime and violence. This makes people feel that it is not safe to come on holiday to the area. The hotels take security very seriously and try to keep local people out. They also like to keep the tourists in, by making the holidays 'all inclusive'. All meals and drinks are included in the price, which discourages tourists from leaving the hotel area and buying things locally.

Tourism helps the building industry

The building industry has benefited greatly from the continuing success of tourism. Air and road transport links are vital to tourism, which means that new roads and airports have had to be built. New hotels have been built and historic buildings have been renovated.

▲ *This hotel in Jamaica is patrolled by security guards and surrounded by high fences topped with barbed wire.*

◄ *The money from increased tourism has helped the Cuban government to restore the beautiful old city of Havana.*

Unemployment and the informal sector

Many people, and in particular men, are unemployed across the Caribbean, despite the new jobs created by the increase in tourism. Some have part-time or seasonal jobs which do not bring in enough money. People have to find whatever work they can so that they can buy food for their families. Some clean windscreens at the traffic lights in towns, others go fishing for food.

Much of this work is part of the informal economy. This means that the jobs are not recognized and people do not pay tax. Many people would not be able to survive without this type of work. Education and training for skilled jobs is very important to help people find well-paid and secure work.

▲ *Training young people in building and engineering skills is an important way to combat unemployment.*

◄ *Women often grow food for their families and sell what is left over at the market.*

IN THEIR OWN WORDS

'I'm Dorette Carty and I am a higgler in Jamaica. 'Higgler' is a Jamaican word for a street trader. I work on this patch for six days a week and go to church on Saturday because I'm a Seventh Day Adventist. My mother had this spot so I took it over from her. I like working here because you can start and finish when you like. I usually work from eight in the morning until six in the evening. I lock my stuff up in the market. I have to keep changing my stock according to the fashion. There's been a big increase in the number of higglers and a lot of competition. Many people have been made redundant from their jobs, so they take up selling on the street.'

Make do and mend

Consumer items like electrical goods are very expensive for people in the Caribbean. When they break, people try to repair them and make them last as long as possible.

Cars on the streets are often quite old and small garages with mechanics are everywhere. Cubans have been unable to buy new cars for decades, because of the US trade embargo which has prevented Cuba from buying foreign goods. The cars there are from the 1950s. This in itself has become something of a tourist attraction.

◀ *Cars dating back to the 1950s are a common sight on the streets of Havana.*

The Way Ahead

The beautiful scenery and sunny climate of the Caribbean are bringing in more money from tourism. But the majority of the population still live in varying degrees of poverty. Many Caribbean countries are heavily in debt to richer countries. The governments need to put money in to new industries and provide education and training in order to build up a skilled workforce. But the money that they need to spend on education and health programmes is being used to pay back their loans from other countries. A solution to this problem would be for the richer countries who lent them the money to cancel the debts.

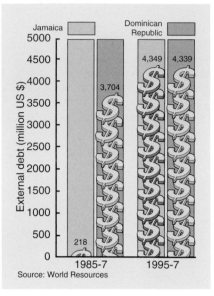

▲ The money these Caribbean islands owe to other countries is still increasing.

◄ The Caribbean is one of the world's most popular holiday destinations, but it will need support from richer countries if it is to be able to provide for its people in the future.

Caribbean countries spend much of their money on importing goods from abroad. They rely on foreign countries to supply them with many consumer goods and foods, such as grain. This is very expensive and they have no control over the prices that they have to pay. The governments in the region have united to form the Caribbean Common Market (Caricom). They hope that together they will be stronger and may be able to solve some of their problems. But they will not be able to overcome their difficulties alone.

The Caribbean will need real support from other countries and it will have to decide which ones to approach. It could approach its nearest neighbour, South America. Or it could draw on its historical ties with the old colonial powers in Europe. Or it could request help from the USA, a country to which it is increasingly bound, both culturally and economically. Given the opportunity to develop itself, the Caribbean could have a future that is bright for all of its people.

▲ *This girl may decide to emigrate if she cannot find work in Jamaica.*

IN THEIR OWN WORDS

'My name is Mayelen Reyes Narenjo. I am 27 years old and I live in Cuba. I am a pharmacy student in my first year at university. Pharmacy is a good degree to have because you qualify as a doctor and it's easy to get a job. The course is hard though – it takes five years to complete and involves a lot of chemistry.

'I'm a bit older than most of the other students. Cuban workers have the right to study. The government will pay anyone under 30 to study and ensure that your job is kept open for you. Many people come here to study because it is much cheaper than in the USA or Europe. I am glad that I live in a country where education is given such importance. I know that I have a good future here.'

Glossary

Ammonia A strong-smelling gas that is a mixture of nitrogen and hydrogen.

Ancestors People who lived before us and to whom we are related, including our grandparents and any relations before them.

Bauxite A clay-like mineral, from which aluminium is made.

Calypso A popular tuneful song about a piece of gossip or an item in the news.

Caustic Chemicals that can destroy or severely damage animals and plants by causing burns.

Colonialism One country takes control of another one and continues to rule over it.

Commonwealth In the case of Puerto Rico, this means that it is an associated territory of the USA and its people are US citizens.

Cultivating Preparing the land and growing crops.

Data-processing Using computers to store and work on large amounts of information, from booking airline tickets to dealing with a company's salaries.

Data systems The network of all channels of communication within an organization.

Deforestation Forest clearance, for timber or so that the land can be used for other purposes.

Democracy A system of government where the people vote for who they want to run the country on their behalf.

Dependency A territory that is governed by a country that is not next to it.

Duty-free No tax is paid.

Economic Relating to the ways in which money is made.

Economy All the business that goes on in a country, including trade with other countries.

Eco-tourism Holidays to experience the beauty of the natural world.

Egret A type of white heron.

Embargo A ban on trade with a particular country, imposed by another country's government.

Emigrant Someone who leaves their country to go and live in another one.

Entrepreneur Somebody who sets up their own business and makes money by having their own ideas or taking chances.

Exports Goods and services that a country sells to other countries.

Geothermal Heat that originates from deep inside the Earth.

Global warming Increases in average world temperatures, thought to be caused by carbon dioxide and some other gases polluting the Earth's atmosphere.

Higglers Women who sell fruit, vegetables and other goods on the streets.

Imports Goods and services that a country buys from other countries.

Income The money a person or country earns.

Life expectancy The average number of years people in a particular region or country are expected to live.

Literacy rate The percentage of adults who have basic reading and writing skills.

Manufacturing industry The business of making goods for sale, such as cars and toys.

Minerals Substances such as coal and bauxite, which occur naturally in the ground and can be obtained by mining.

Mulch Anything spread on the ground around the roots of a plant to keep the moisture in the soil.

Nationalized An industry that is controlled by the government, instead of being run by private companies.

Nitrates Fertilizers containing nitrate salts.

Phosphate A chemical used as a detergent and water softener.

Plantation A large area of land that is planted with a single crop or type of tree.

Rift valley A valley with steep sides, formed by a split in the Earth's crust.

Run-off Water that flows over the earth because the ground cannot absorb it.

Rural Relating to the countryside.

Scarlet ibis A wading bird found in Trinidad.

Shanty town A poor area on the outskirts of a town or city where people have built homes out of scrap materials.

Slavery Forcing people to work for little or no money. Slaves belong to their owners and can be bought and sold.

Social security Money that the government gives to people who are poor or unemployed.

Tectonic plates The plates of the Earth's crust. These plates move very slowly, which can cause earthquakes and create volcanoes where the plates meet.

Trade winds Steady winds that blow from the north-east toward the Equator.

Urban Built-up area, such as a town or city.

Vendors People who sell things.

Further Information

Useful addresses

Bannana Link,
8a Guildhall Hill,
Norwich NR2 1JG
Tel. 01603 765670
Website: www.bananalink.org.uk

Latin American Bureau,
1 Amwell Street,
London EC1R 1UL
Tel. 020 7278 2829
Website: www.lab.org.uk

Oxfam Education,
274 Banbury Road,
Oxford OX2 7DZ
Tel. 01865 311 311
Website: www.oxfam.org.uk/coolplanet/

Teaching pack

Go Bananas, Oxfam

Video

Landmarks: Caribbean Islands, BBC, 2001. Three programmes exploring life on the islands of Triniddad and Dominica.

Map

Caribbean Map, Oxfam

Books
Fiction

Anancy and Other Stories, audiocassette, Blue Mountain Media, 1998. Caribbean stories told in West India patois with music and sound effects. Also available in paperback.

A Caribbean Dozen, Walker Books, 1996. An illustrated collection of poems by 13 Caribbean authors.

Give Yourself A Hug, Grace Nichols, Puffin Books, 1996. Illustrated poetry collection.

The Island Hopping Game, Barbara Applin, Caribbean Publishing, 2000.

Non-fiction

Traditional Stories from the Caribbean, Petronella Breinburg, Hodder Wayland, 2006

Festivals and Food: The Caribbean, Linda Illsley, Hodder Wayland, 2006

Country Files: The Caribbean, Ian Graham, Franklin Watts, 2005

The Landscape of St Lucia, Alison Brownlie, Hodder Wayland, 2001

The People of St Lucia, Alison Brownlie, Hodder Wayland, 2001

Useful websites

BBC Education: The Windrush Files at
www.bbc.co.uk/schools/teachers/ks3
/historymulticultural.shtml
CIA World Factbook at
www.odci.gov/cia/publications/factbook
United Nations Children's Fund (UNICEF) at
www.unicef.org
United Nations Development Programme (UNDP)
at www.undp.org

Index

Numbers in **bold** are pages where there is a photograph or an illustration.

Africa 6, 7, **7**, 20, **20**, **21**, 23, 31, 32, 33
air transport 16, **25**, 41
alternative energy 14, **14**
animals 16, **38**, 41
Antigua **5**, **12**
Arawaks 6

bananas 9, 38, 39, **39**
Barbados 5, **5**, 13, 15, 35, 40
bauxite 13, **13**, 19, **19**, 34
building work 16, 18, 41, **41**
business 12, 21, 34, 35, **35**, 39

Caribs 6
carnivals 4
cars 12, 13, **16**, 43, **43**
children 9, **10**, 21, **21**, 23, **23**, 26, 27, 28, **28**, **29**, 31, 33, **38**
cities 4, **4**, 5, **5**, **16**, **17**, 21, **21**, 23, **23**, 24, **24**, 25, 26, **27**, 32, 33, 35, 37, 40, **40**, **41**, **43**
climate 10-11, **10-11**
clothes 26, 27, 36, 37
coasts, coastal plains 8, 10, **10**, 40, 41
coffee 9, 29, **29**, 38, **38**
colonialism 6, 30, 45
communities 25, 27, 32, **32**, 33
  theatre 4
computers 35, **35**
  games 27, 30
coral 15, 17
crime 33, 41
crops 9, 11, 18, 38-9, **38-9**
Cuba 4, **4**, 5, **5**, 7, **7**, 8, 10, **17**, 20, **20**, 21, 22, 23, **23**, 25, 26, 27, **27**, 28, **30**, 31, **31**, 32, **32**, 38, 40, **40**, 41, **41**, 43, **43**, 45, **45**
culture 4, 6, 20, 27, 31, **31**, 45

deforestation 11, 17, 18
Dominica **5**, 8, 22
Dominican Republic **5**, 10, 14, 24, 28, 35, 36

economy 7, 34, 35, 42, 45
education 21, 22, 23, 24, 25, 28, 37, 42, 44, 45
elderly 22, **22**, 28
English 5, 30, 32
Europe, Europeans 6, 7, 24, 25, 27, 31, 34, 39, 40, 45
exports 12, 13, 38, 39

factories 12, 16, 26, 34, 36, **36**, 37
families 11, 22, 24, 25, 28-9, 33, 38, 39, 42
farming, farmland 16, 17, 19, **19**, 29, **29**, 34, 37, **37**, 38-9, **38-9**
fashion 26, 40
fish 15, 17, 29
flags **4**
food 7, 15, 18, 20, 29, **29**, 36, 42
France, French 5, 21, 32, 40
free trade zone 15, 26, 36, **36**, 37, **37**
fruit 9, 29, 38, 39

Grenada **5**, 35
Guadeloupe **5**, 8
Guyana **5**, 8, 12, 13, 14, 20

Haiti 4, **5**, 6, **6**, 10, 11, **11**, 18, **18**, 22, 23, **23**, 25, 26, 28, **29**, 32, 37, 38, **38**
Havana **4**, 7, **17**, 21, 40, **40**, **41**, 43
health 22, 23, 29, 44
history 6-7, **6-7**, 39, 45
holidays (see also tourism) 4, 41
hotels 16, 17, 34, 40, **40**, 41, **41**

imports **12**, 43
independence 5, 6, **6**, 7
India 6, 20
industry, industrialization 12, 16, 19, **19**, 24, 34, 36, **36**, 37, 38, 41, **41**

Jamaica 4, 5, **5**, **9**, **11**, 12, **12**, 13, **13**, 15, **15**, **16**, 19, **19**, 20, 21, **21**, 24, 25, **25**, 26, **26**, **30**, **31**, 32, 33, **33**, 34, 35, **35**, 36, 37, **37**, 39, **39**, 40, 41, **41**, 43, **43**, **45**

Kingston 4, 5, **5**, **16**, 21, 24, 25, 26, 33, 35, 37

landscape 8-9, **8-9**, 19, **19**
language 5, 6, 31
lifestyles 4, 23, 27

migration 24-5, 45
mines, mining 12, 19, **19**, 34
money 16, 23, 25, 26, 29, 40, 41, 42, 44, 45
Montserrat **5**, 8
mountains 8, **8**, 9, **9**, 10
music 26, 31, **31**

oil 12-13, 14, 15, 24, 34

plantations 6, 7, 20, 21, 29, **29**, 38, **38**, 39, **39**
plants 16, 19, 41

pollution 15, 16, **16**, 17, **17**
population 5, 8, 20-25, **20-25**, 26, 29, 33, 38, 40, 44
  growth 15, 16, 22
Port of Spain 4, **5**
poverty, poor 4, 18, 22, 23, 26, 28, 33, 44
Puerto Rico 4, 5, **5**, 6, 7, 12, 14, 16, 20, 21, 25, 34

rain 8, 9, 10, **10**, 11, 18
rainforests 8, 17, 18
Rastafarian 32, 33, **33**
religion 5, 6, 20, 32, 43
rivers 8, 14, 17
roads 11, 16, 41

St Kitts and Nevis **5**, **24**, 35
St Lucia 4, **5**, 8, **8**, 14, **14**, 24, 31, 36, **36**, 38, 39, 40
St Vincent **5**, 8, 10, 24, 39
San Juan 4, 5, **5**, 24
school (see also education) 28, **28**, 29
sea **5**, 8, 15, 17, **17**, 18
shopping malls 4, **27**, 33, 40
slaves, slavery 4, 6, **6**, 7, **7**, 20, 31
South America 8, 45
Spain, Spanish 5, 7, 20, **20**, 21, 31, 32, 40
sport 4, 30, **30**
sugar 6, 7, 20, 21, 24, 38
Suriname **5**, 8
swamps 8, 16

Taínos 6
technology 30, 34, **34**, 35, **35**
television 26, 27, 30, 31, 32
tourism, tourists **7**, 10, 15, 16, 17, 27, 31, 34, 35, 40-41, **40-41**, 42, 43, 44
Trinidad and Tobago 4, **5**, 11, 12, 13, 20, **28**, 31, 32, 34, 35

unemployment 25, 33, 36, 42
USA **5**, 7, 25, 26, 27, 30, 31, 34, 35, 36, 39, 40, 43, 45

vegetables 9, 11
volcanoes, volcanic rock 8, **8**, 13, **13**, 14, **14**

women 22, **22**, 28, 29, **29**, 32, 36, 37, **37**, **42**
work, workers 6, 7, 9, **9**, 12, 15, **15**, 16, 17, **17**, 18, **18**, 19, 20, 21, 23, **23**, 24, 25, **25**, 28, 29, **29**, 33, 34-43, **34-43**, 45, **45**